# EXPOSE
# *and* CLOSE

*Simple Networking, Marketing and Sales
Techniques to Activate, Acquire, and Achieve
Massive Success*

# Charlie Cina

Dedicated To:

The love of my life, Tennille, and our two incredible kids,
Carmen and Sophia.

Thank you for your unconditional love and support.

And
in memory of my extraordinary friend,
Carl 'Big Vini' Bergemen.

Expose
& Close
Marketing System

www.exposeandclose.com

I t was spring of 1987. I was a 20-year-old kid in Las Vegas with scholarships to finish up at UNLV with a degree in Hotel Restaurant Management. I was living with my girlfriend's older brother Rich, who decided to buy a limousine and get into the limo business. The day his new 72-foot stretch Lincoln Town Car was delivered into his driveway was the day I met Big Vini.

Vini delivered the new white Lincoln stretch limo in a parade-like procession — his personal 35-foot black Lincoln stretch he named Darth Vader followed in tow. As my buddy's new limo approached the driveway, the windows and dual moon roofs opened up and beautiful girls popped out shouting congratulations to Rich. Our entourage of friends that were there to be a part of the festivities all jumped into the new limo but there was no room for me.

No big deal. I said, "I'll hang here and see you guys when you get back."

As the limo pulled away, I found myself looking at Darth Vader and a 5-foot 10-inch, 260-pound man with a full black beard who was wearing more gold jewelry than Mr. T. He stuck out his hand and said in a heavy New York accent, "Hi. My name is Vini. What's your name?"

Now mind you, I didn't know if this guy was a limo builder or a hitman from New York, so I really didn't want to give him my name. However, with the situation I was in — just me, Vini, and his 6-foot plus driver named Rocky — I felt like I didn't have a choice.

I stuck out my hand and replied, "My name is Charlie."

He said, "Charlie what?"

I said, "Charlie Cina."

"Cina," he said. "You Italian?" "Yes," I replied.

"Me too. My last name is Bergeman. My father was Dutch and my Mom's Italian. Where you from?" he asked.

"New York," I replied.

With a smile, Vini said, "Me too. What part of New York?"

"Buffalo," I said.

With a grin and his finger pointed to his chest, he proudly said, "Bronx. I'm from the Bronx." Then, without any hesitation, he looked at me dead in the eye and said, "Charlie, I like you. I can tell you're a good kid. We're going to be friends for a long time."

I didn't realize it at that moment, but in less than one minute of conversation I had unconsciously learned two of the most valuable life lessons from Big Vini. Lesson one, the power of your name, and lesson two, the power of the C word ... 'commitment'.

Vini looked at me and said, "We're going out tonight and you'll be riding in first class with me."

Who would have thought one intimidating introduction would have resulted in a 30-year relationship of a best friend? And what a ride it was! These simple yet dynamic lessons would help me advance as a sales professional, entrepreneur, friend, and mentor.

'Big Vini' The Original Kustomizer

# Contents

Foreword by Joel Bauer ...........................................................XI

Introduction ............................................................................ 1

## EXPOSE YOUR BRAND

Expose, Expose, Expose! ..................................................... 11

Be a Disciple of Sales........................................................... 15

The Power of Your Name ....................................................... 19

Name Leverage ..................................................................... 23

Differentiation with a Brand Called U ................................... 29

It's All in the Packaging ........................................................ 33

The Best Calling Card ........................................................... 39

## POWERFUL WORDS AND MINDSETS

Words are Things .................................................................. 44

The "C" Word......................................................................... 48

Time: Tomorrow is Promised to Nobody................................ 52

Certainty: A Sales Professional's #1 Job ............................. 58

Intention and Attention.......................................................... 64

Clients vs. Customers............................................................ 68

# When You Expose ... You Close!

You Gotta Move ........................................................... 75

Organic Money Opportunities ................................. 79

The Show Up.............................................................. 85

The Knock .................................................................. 89

The Cold Call is Not Dead........................................ 93

Direct Mail is so "Out" It's "In"................................ 99

The Drop Off.............................................................. 105

Video Follow Up ........................................................ 109

# Exposure Tips And Techniques

Send a Note, Send a Card, Send a Pizza ............... 119

Social Media and Facebook..................................... 125

Voicemail and Text Messages ................................ 131

Million Dollar Messengers ....................................... 135

Nothing Falls on Deaf Ears .................................... 143


Conclusion - There's No Silver Bullet .................... 149

Resources ................................................................. 153

Thought Leaders, Influencers and Mentors ........... 157

www.exposeandclose.com

# Foreword by Joel Bauer

I had been behind the scenes in seclusion preparing for a massive event. Then I get Charlie Cina's book *Expose and Close* in the mail. I receive numerous books every month from students, colleagues and business associates, but unfortunately, I do not have time to read them all. I opened *Expose and Close,* and after going through the table of contents, it hooked me. I started to engage in Charlie's book and as much as I wanted to put it aside, I couldn't.

I know this man, I know about his ethical and moral fabric, his manifesto for life and his intentions. Charlie Cina is an expert in sales, an expert at closing, and an expert on manifesting relationships that sustain. I have to tell you that Charlie is a man of integrity and he's passionate about his profession. He has never lied to me and he has never distorted. Charlie is an amazing human being with a passion and purpose for helping people take their lives to the next level.

I just couldn't put this book down. It was like I picked something on Netflix and next thing you know you're binge-watching. This book is all consuming and you will see there's brilliance behind it. But what's really behind this book is experience, with tried-and-true techniques that can be transferred and learned. Take the time to dive in and read this book cover to cover. Then read it again and again and implement Charlie's techniques.

This book builds wealth. If you take three techniques from this book, just three and you use them, your results are going to be staggering. You just need to implement what he simply lays out step by step.

You need this book.

Joel Bauer
The Mentor's Mentor

# Introduction

Hi. My name is Charlie Cina, and for the past 30 years, I have worked in high-level sales environments building sales teams and driving revenue. I have started my own seven-figure businesses by doing nothing more than shaking hands, knocking on doors, and utilizing my cell phone. I have profited in industries including automotive, retail, software, construction, promotions, and numerous others.

I have had the privilege to master sales and sell into billion-dollar hotel and casino projects like Wynn Las Vegas, The Palazzo Las Vegas, Mandarin Oriental Las Vegas, and MGM Grand. I have collaborated and worked with companies like Pepsi, Barrett-Jackson Auto Auction, and Discovery Channel.

In 2012, I entered the world of virtual interactive training. This new arena of business has allowed me to recruit and work with the top motivational speakers, sales trainers, and subject matter experts in the world. I have personally consulted and guided them in the creation of their interactive online training platforms that deliver their content and monetize worldwide. My tried-and-true sales and marketing techniques have allowed me to acquire clients like Les Brown, Tony Robbins, Jon Taffer, 'The Cake Boss' Buddy Valastro, Eric Thomas, and a list of others equally talented in their own fields.

My objective for writing this book is to teach you that no matter what products or services you represent, we all have one thing in common. We are all in the distribution business and your primary responsibility is to expose your brand, expose your products, expose your services, expose your message, and expose your solutions, so that you may ultimately close more deals and drive massive revenue.

Over 40 years ago, unbeknownst to me, I was starting my sales career as a paperboy in Buffalo, New York. I dragged my paper wagon through the snow on cold winter days, knocking on doors to increase my distribution. My goal was making sure the paper was always on time — fresh and unwrinkled — to ensure my clients received a quality product. I learned at a very young age that you produce more when you introduce more.

Now, I wasn't born with a silver spoon in my mouth. However, I did watch and experience my dad take his family from a modest lifestyle to a lifestyle that became incredible. My dad provided everything you could imagine for my mom, my sister, and me. My dad was an entrepreneur, a consummate networker, and sales professional. He had an innate ability to commit, implement, and go all in with any venture he believed had the opportunity to produce revenue.

And here's the crazy part ... dad had nothing more than a 9th-grade education, yet he afforded us the biggest and best house on the street. We had Cadillacs, Bentleys, vacations, and an in-ground pool in the backyard. I remember huge birthday parties and Christmases that were unforgettable.

Then, it all came to a screeching halt. I watched my dad's fortune crumble. He lost his businesses, revenue streams, and investments, which ultimately ended in a divorce between him and my mother. I personally think divorce is second to death.

The breakup of a family unit is difficult for all parties, no matter what the situation and no matter who is right or who is wrong.

So, growing up living a privileged lifestyle and seeing it fall apart had instilled in me a fear of poverty; a fear of not being able to provide for myself; a fear of not creating, attaining, and maintaining a family; and a fear I may not be able to start my own business or have significance in this marketplace that is ultimately called life.

Fortunately for me, I experienced and learned the essential skill sets, techniques, and formulas to generate revenue. These skill sets were not taught to me in school or in college. However, I was fortunate enough to learn some essential sales, networking, and personal skills from my father, both of my grandfathers, and through caring strangers who ultimately became my mentors. My mentors taught me their techniques and transferred their skill sets to me, helping me take my life to another level.

## The Reality Check

As I write this book, the current financial opportunities for millennials in the United States looks very dismal. I'm not being a pessimist; I'm being a realist.

Here are the facts:

- Over 70 percent of millennials have less than $1,000 in the bank.

- The average millennial is over $21,000 in debt.

- Millennials carry 100 percent more debt than their Gen-Y parents.

- The average income for a millennial employee is $35,592 a year.

- Millennials collectively share $1,000,000,000+ of

student debt.

- 48 percent of employed college graduates work in jobs that don't require a 4-year degree.

If you look at the average American, their financial situation is not any better.

The average median income in the United States as of 2017 is $56,516. That's not much when you really take a hard look at it. The average credit card debt is about $5,700. If you are in your 30s and you combine that with student loan debt, you're looking at an average debt of over $34,000. But wait … it gets worse! The sad part is, 73 percent of Americans are dying with an average of $62,000 worth of debt. This is insane!

People bust their asses going to school and come out of college behind the eight ball with tremendous debt. Then comes the cars, a house, second mortgages, marriage, babies, more expenses, and more debt. How do you possibly have more money at the end of a month instead of more month at the end of the money? Common? I know you've heard that one before, but this is a very true reality.

So many of us have been conditioned to be on the program of 'dollars earned for time spent.' People look for jobs with a high hourly wage and, those that hustle, pray for some over- time so they can get time-and-a-half. Others strive and set a goal to find a great job which means a comfortable salary with benefits.

Now, I am not cutting anybody down for wanting to find a good J.O.B. to work and feed their family. However, it is crystal clear with over 73 percent of the country dying with debt, this formula is a recipe for disaster. Let me give you an example.

I asked my trainer one day why I was not losing weight. I told her, "I am in the gym every day killing myself and sometimes I work out twice a day. Why can't I drop weight?"

She replied, "Charlie, it doesn't matter how hard you work in the gym because you can't outwork a bad diet." I was consuming more calories than I was burning. Simple math.

The point I am trying to impress upon you is you cannot stay ahead of the curve by trying to work more hours for more pay. Keeping up with inflation, the price of cars, food, and etc. is almost impossible. You can try to live your life by working more hours while trying to reduce your expenses or going without, but that is a piss poor formula or, in this case, a very bad financial diet. Therefore, let me tell you a little secret which is really a reality check. Are you ready?

You don't have expense or debt problems ... you have income problems. That's right — you have an income problem. You need more income — more revenue. "Why?" you ask. BECAUSE REVENUE FIXES EVERYTHING.

## What is Money?

Money is not everything, however, money IS leverage. Money takes away stress. Money helps you find a resolution to most problems — or at least increases your options to solve problems. Money allows you to help those that are not as privileged, educated, or skilled. Money helps you support and/or donate to those that do not have the abilities to support themselves. Money is not the root of all evil. Money — with the right intentions — can make a difference in your life; make a difference in the lives of people you love; and ultimately allows you to give back to your community, church, and charities you wish to help.

In my pursuit of financial success, I have struggled, fought, tripped, fallen, and — on a couple of occasions –lost it all. Fortunately, I learned how to overcome numerous adversities in my life by having the ability to reinvent myself through a skill we call sales or selling. I want to transfer all the tried and true techniques, formulas, systems, and word tracks to help you overcome your revenue pain.

Remember, you don't have expense problems, you have revenue problems and REVENUE fixes everything.

We all suffer when we do not know, or when we are not prepared. Therefore, it's my intention to help you present yourself in a way that's unforgettable. Whether you're knocking on doors or you're on a stage; whether you're presenting to an individual, to the public, or to a corporate entity, I will help you position yourself as the only logical choice. I want to teach you the skills that will transfer your message and expose your truth, authenticity, and proof. These techniques will potentially help you profit in ways you never thought possible by generating revenue relationships and creating multiple revenue streams.

Through this book, it's my intention to save you from a 20 to 30-year learning curve. I intend to help you expose, close, and create a business and lifestyle of your own design. What I am about to transfer to you are my proven techniques, word tracks, formulas, and a HOW TO, STEP-BY-STEP SYSTEM that works to MakeSalesEasy.com.

I want to give you a path that demystifies the secrets of successful salespeople in business and provides insight to help you achieve your goals.

Now, allow me to introduce some tried and true proven systems and techniques that will teach you how to EXPOSE, CLOSE, AND DRIVE MASSIVE REVENUE. Let's get started.

We all have what it takes, but it's up to us
to find our purpose and put it into action.

**8**    Expose and Close

# Expose Your Brand

# Expose, Expose, Expose!

I use the word 'expose' to replace the word 'marketing'. Many people out there — whether they are in sales, own a business, provide a service, or are looking for a J.O.B. — don't seem to realize that they must market themselves. They are intimidated by the word 'marketing' and it's a fact that even more are intimidated by the word 'sales'. So, I like the word 'EXPOSE'.

Although that word today may trigger some negative connotations, it definitely gets attention and I am obviously not afraid to use it. You see, EXPOSE means marketing, promoting, piquing interest, exhibiting brand awareness, and essentially telling people who you are, what you do, what problems you can help them solve, or how you can make their lives better. You should be exposing you, your company, your services, your customer testimonials, your brand, and your products and services 24/7 on demand to anyone and everyone you meet. It is a very simple skill that can be learned and, more importantly, taught.

These skills are not just for your business, they are for your life. They will help you acquire and build new relationships, advance relationships, network, build your brand, build your value, and help you build your bank account.

Mary Kay Ash who started and created a multibillion-dollar company said that for anything to work, you have to ask yourself:

- Is it simple?
- Does it work?
- Can I do this?

I am here to tell you that every one of the chapters written in this book is based on my personal implementation and life experience. These tactics and technics work for me every day of my life. They have worked for my clients, family members, business associates, and friends and they WILL work for you. These tactics are simple, they have generated me millions of dollars, and they absolutely, positively work. Now read on, retain the info, and take action.

Present yourself in a way that is unforgettable, so people will say, "I want what you have to offer."

Making money is the direct result
of success, not the other way around.

# Be a Disciple of Sales

S ales is the highest paying profession in the world … bar none. Many of today's top business tycoons, millionaires, and billionaires started in a sales position. They learned the essential skills of inspiring, motivating, and persuading people to take action and engage in a financial transaction.

Everything is related to selling. Sales is the absolute most essential skill that a person must acquire to really make a financial difference in their life. We are all salespeople and, whether you realize it or not, YOU are a salesperson. You are an influencer. You inspire and you have persuaded hundreds, if not thousands, of people to make decisions. And the decisions were all based upon words you have said and things you have demonstrated or communicated through body language to get people to buy into your thoughts, ideas, and/or get them to make some kind of transaction.

My son and daughter have been excellent salespeople since the time they were able to communicate. I remember when they would see a toy on TV or in a magazine. They would say, "Dad I want this?" Immediately, innately, and almost magically, their natural instincts of salesmanship were turned on. They had identified their 'why' — their goal, their target — and could only think about achieving it. They became obsessed with obtaining the result. They became relentless by constantly saying, "I want this! When can we go to the store?" They would leave me notes, drawings, or any other form of communication they could think of that would influence me to buy them that toy.

Their follow-up skills were incredible. Their passion and justification of why they should have that toy is something that I still remember. I wish I could have bottled their enthusiasm and fearlessness into a pill. They were determined, not worrying about the NO or the rejection. They were motivated, inspired, took constant action, exuded confidence and persistence, and practiced relentless follow up. Their reasoning and justification were on a high emotional level of why they wanted and deserved that toy.

So, as I mentioned earlier, we are all salespeople. It is a survival instinct inside all of us that allows us to communicate, negotiate, inspire, justify, and ultimately persuade other individuals to come over to our side or to get our way or what we want.

We sell when we convince somebody to go to a restaurant we like. We sell or persuade others to go on the first date. Then we must continue to influence, persuade, and exude emotional confidence to get the second date, third date ... and ultimately ask the question, "Will you marry me?"

When my son wants to go to the mall to buy a new pair of sneakers, all the attributes of his sales abilities come out. The sneakers are his 'why'. They are the motivation and inspiration that automatically makes him exude confidence, persistence, and relentless reasoning of why he needs the sneakers or why he deserves them.

We are all salespeople. Some of us have more talent than others, however, these talents can be enhanced. Sales skills — or better yet the art of presentation — can be taught, transferred, and learned with the right mentor.

It is your time to educate yourself … to elevate yourself. When you educate and elevate you become a disciple of sales. You will dominate your space and you will generate incredible opportunities and revenue you never thought possible. When you become a disciple of sales and master the art of presentation, you can write your own ticket. You can decide what product you want to represent, how many hours you want to work, and where you want to live.

Sales is not a profession of dollars earned for time spent. You do not trade your time for dollars. You become a pseudo partner of the company and product you're representing. You increase your revenue stream by receiving a percentage of everything you bring in. There is nothing more exciting or motivating than the reality of knowing the more you produce the more you're going to receive. Just make sure you jump on the right sales vehicle that will allow you to have no ceiling on what you can earn.

When you're a sales professional, you will never be out of work. When you become a true professional, you will be sought after by many who will want you to help them distribute their products, thus driving MASSIVE revenues to their company.

Marketing, sales, and the ability to persuade are prerequisites of life.

# The Power of Your Name

The first thing we are given or gifted when we come into the world is a name. Your life is a gift — a miracle actually. It's a 400 trillion:1 shot that YOU were created. But, let's not forget the gift you were given when your parents gave you a NAME. Parents spend a great deal of time thinking and consulting family members and friends about what they should call God's new creation ... that new creation that will soon be their son or daughter.

A name is a word and, as we discussed, words are things. Words trigger pictures in your mind. Those pictures trigger emotions. Those emotions create perceptions — either positive or negative. That's why it is so important to be conscious and aware of the words you speak.

The definition of the word name is: a word or phrase that constitutes the distinctive designation of a person or thing. Notice the key word in that definition is 'distinctive'. What makes you distinctive? What in your persona makes you stand out? What is your differentiator — the thing or things that make you unique and memorable? What about you gives people the feeling or need to want to talk with you, be in your company, laugh with you, do business with you, or have a personal relationship with you?

The power in you exposing your name and the power in using someone's name should be utilized and leveraged throughout your entire life.

Your name is your brand. It is no different than when you say a brand name like Coca-Cola. When I say Coca-Cola, what does that mean to you? What pictures are triggered and what emotions do you feel? When I hear Coca-Cola, I think pizza, hamburgers, BBQs, family, friends, ballgames, and parties. I think of the billion-dollar company and its international appeal that is a part of Americana.

Your name is your brand. It stands for who you are, what you believe in, how you are perceived, and what people can expect from you. Your name is something that everyone needs to know. It is your call sign in audio, video, and written format. It is reflected on your billboard of life.

One of the first things you learn to write is your name. You put it on your school assignments to be identified, graded, and recognized for the work you do. It is one of the first things you say when making a presentation, introduction, or speech. Think about the famous singer Johnny Cash. As simplistic as it was, he was known for opening every show with, "Hello. My name is Johnny Cash." He did it when he was starting as a nobody and continued this throughout his career. That was his brand, his call sign — 'Johnny Cash', 'The Man in Black', 'A Boy Named Sue' — a country music legend and an American icon.

When people hear your name enough, they will seek to know your face. When they recognize your face, they will seek to find out who you really are. If you're authentic and they like who you are, you will build solid and long-term relationships. These relationships will open other doors and create new opportunities. These are the friendships that will help shape and direct your life.

Success is the difference between
my potential and my reality.

www.exposeandclose.com

# Name Leverage

How you leverage your name is important and everyone need to know your name. So, here is a million-dollar move. Every day you should go up to 10 strangers and say these magic words. "Hi. My name is_____. What's your name?"

It seems like such a small minute tactic; however, few people master what should be common sense and a gesture of common courtesy. I always think back to the day I met Big Vini. As intimidating as I thought Vini was, he completely defused my initial negative judgment when he said, "Hi. My name is Vini. What's your name?"

As soon as I heard his name and I told him my name, something miraculous happened. We were not strangers anymore. Questions were asked, a conversation flowed, and a relationship immediately started to form and build.

It is bothersome to me why it is easier to say, "Goodbye," than it is to say, "Hello." However, once a relationship is formed, the goodbyes become harder. Unfortunately, most people fear rejection — it's part of human nature. But when you master the common courtesy tactic of, "Hi. What's your name?" doors will open in your personal and business life.

After watching Vini in numerous business meetings, and in social and personal settings, I concluded the real formula is telling people your name first and then asking for their name. I have experimented with this for years and here are a couple examples that brought me to this conclusion.

My family and I were out to dinner at a Japanese Teppan restaurant. There was a family sitting across from us and I was sitting directly across from a 10-year-old boy. I said, "Hi. What's your name?"

He put his head down and did not respond. I asked him a second time. Again, no response. The third time I said, "My name is Charlie. What's your name?"

He immediately responded, "My name is Taylor."

"Taylor, nice to meet you. How old are you?"

He responded, "Ten years old," and the questions and conversation just kept flowing.

When people know your name first their guard comes down and their trust levels goes up. Although this is very entry level, it immediately establishes a common ground that can turn into a life-long friendship.

When I traveled with Big Vini, I noticed that everyone he met was important and significant. I watched him do business with celebrities — who he always made feel important — but he was just as interested and courteous to the waitress at Denny's. No matter who was in his presence, he would make a friend, talk about his business, and leave a positive impression on the person he just befriended.

Try addressing people by their name and watch what happens. Go into a restaurant and you'll notice the little 1-inch by 3-inch piece of plastic that the hostess, waitress, and pretty much every staff member is wearing. It has their name on it. Why? So, customers know who they are talking to. However, that hostess or waitress almost never introduces themselves, nor does the customer usually try to call the waitress by name.

I can't stand when I hear someone call a waitress, hostess, or retail clerk 'Hon', 'Babe', 'Ma'am', or any other lazy slang names. They have a name and so do you … USE IT! If they do not introduce themselves when you're in their establishment, you must introduce yourself to them. When I go into a restaurant, clothing store, government facility like the DMV, or any establishment for that matter, I do one very simple thing … if the person I'm dealing with is wearing a name tag I use it and say, "Hi Katie. I'm Charlie. How are you? I was wondering if you can help me out. I'm here for a new suit today," or, "I'm here to get a new license today." It is a simple gesture of courtesy that immediately opens a clearer level of communication and trust that will result in a better, faster, and more pleasant experience.

Try it. Go to a restaurant and when the waitress or waiter walks up to the table, introduce yourself and call them by name. As a matter of fact, if you are with other people, introduce them to everyone at the table. I have taught my kids to do this since they were old enough to talk. Introduce yourself, ask people their name and then call them by THEIR NAME.

The most pleasant sound a person will ever hear is their name. When you show enough respect to ask people that question in a sincere and genuine manner, your life experience will change. The common decency to build a relationship with a waitress or waiter that you will be interacting with for the next 30 minutes to 2 hours will have a dramatic impact on how you are served. When you know their name and they know yours, you now have a relationship.

Here's an example: Katie the waitress is serving the people at Table 5, but she does not know who they are. The people at Table 8 — Charlie, Tennille, Carmen, and Sophia — they are Katie's new friends. Why? Because Katie knows their names. As a result, Charlie and his family will become regulars and Katie will be paying extra close attention to make sure they always leave happy.

I am here to tell you this works. I have traveled to countries where I didn't speak the language. However, when you know someone's name and they know yours, human acts of kindness will immediately begin to take over. People will know you care, and they will show you their appreciation in ways you never expected. Remember this old adage, "People don't care how much you know until they know how much you care."

You are your competitive advantage.

www.exposeandclose.com

# Differentiation with a Brand Called U

Vini was the most unorganized detail guy I have ever met. He was usually going in a million directions at once with no set plan. However, when it came down to promoting and marketing, he was a detail genius — even down to the spelling of his first name, Vini.

Vini was not spelled V I N N Y like most of the world spells Vinny. It was spelled V I N I. You may have thought this was a typo in the book, but it's not. You see, everybody spells Vinny the traditional way, but Vini wanted to stand out, make noise, start a conversation and it worked. Why? Because your brand reflects who you are and what you represent.

Your name immediately links you to the first impression you make when you shake somebody's hand. When you met Vini — the bearded, hyper, interesting, creative character — you became intrigued and wanted to know more about him, his products, and what he was about.

Your name represents and delivers a perception you give to the other person when you introduce yourself and expose your persona. When you hand someone a business card, say hello at a party, and exchange information, what is your VINI differentiator?

One differentiator I use is an extra thick business card made with 32-point cardstock. When I hand it to people, I watch them try to separate the card because they think I handed them two cards. Guess what happens? It starts another conversation that continues to build a relationship with my new friend. I have just left another impression on this person that I am different — I'm at another level. If my business card looks world class, what does that say about me, my company, my product, my services?

Many people today, especially millennials, say that business cards are outdated. I beg to differ! I have started numerous conversations simply by handing a business card to someone and saying nothing. Now they have my card, they know my name, and, most importantly, they know what I do. I have gotten their attention and 'exposed' my brand to a new friend or prospect. My information and my message to market computes with that person in five seconds or less, triggering questions and ideas on how we can do business together.

I know we have iPhones, digital cards, Facebook, Twitter, and BLAH, BLAH, BLAH, but too many people get lost in technology. Remember, human beings have five senses: sight, smell, hearing, taste, and touch. I will explain my point by using our 6th sense — which hopefully most of us have — which is COMMON sense.

Most people like to engage so we must implement both high-tech and high-touch. Give them a reason to engage and a relationship will build and take on a life of its own. You must make it a point to study, understand, and implement the basic courtesies of human connection. This will give you a big edge in life — especially when a connection is made with truth and authenticity.

There is no point in trying to be somebody else
because everybody else is already taken.

www.exposeandclose.com

# It's All in the Packaging

Perception is reality. I'll say it again. Perception is reality. That means, how people see you is how you really are — at least in the minds of those analyzing, judging, and perceiving you. If a person thinks you're nasty based on the way you look, then you're nasty to them. If a person thinks you're a slob based on how you dress, then you're a slob to them in their eyes.

How do people see you? Do you smile at people? Do you make eye contact when you speak to them? Do you dress appropriately so you make an impression? A positive impression? Remember, what you wear, how you speak, smell, and look is important. It is another reflection of your brand — who you are.

When people see you, hear your name, or see your name, that will immediately trigger a picture that triggers an emotional perception. That's why I am a firm believer in making sure you dress to impress or, as Joel Bauer, The Mentor's Mentor says, "Wrap the package."

I try to dress well and look good. I really don't do it for any- one but me because when I look good, I feel good. When I am dressed, I produce better, feel confident, and feel more accomplished. I also receive much more positive attention and respect. Let's face it, everyone likes a compliment, and everyone likes to feel significant.

My father was in the clothing business when I was a kid, so I have always appreciated nice clothes. Ever since I could remember, my Dad was always dressed in the finest suits with French cuff shirts, cufflinks, a tie, matching pocket square, and always had on a great pair of Italian scarpes — which means shoes in Italian. He used to say, "Son, you can have on the nicest clothes in the world, but it all boils down to the scarpes. You can tell the caliber of a man by his scarpes. You see son, you dress from the bottom up and the shoes are the foundation."

Now maybe I'm going too deep, but I assure you that wrapping your package works. If I am at a conference, in a restaurant, or on a plane or a train, people come up to me and ask me what business I'm in, or if I'm having a good day, or if I live in town or am I just visiting? This is a positive reflection of my brand that gets me attention and exposure. It is also a form of marketing because you can cross paths with hundreds or thousands of people a day who look at you and who you make an impression on.

Dressing well and representing your brand starts conversations. Dressing well lets people know you are a pro and you exude confidence. Dressing well shows respect for all the people you come in contact with.

Try walking into a restaurant wrapped in some nice cloth versus a guy in a T-shirt and shorts. See who gets the better table — or better yet, even gets a table. Hop on a plane and when the flight attendant says, "Nice jacket," watch who gets better service and even gets asked to step into first class. Whenever I travel you will never find me in shorts and T-shirt or workout clothes and sneakers. I wrap the package.

When I walk into a hotel and step to the front desk, I look the front desk clerk in the eye and say, "Hi. I'm Charlie. What's your name?"

She replies, "Susan."

"Susan, the last name is Cina. I'm checking in. Can you help me out?"

Now, this is really simple.

- I said, "Hello."
- I called her by name.
- I politely asked her to help me out and get me checked in.
- I showed up to her hotel property dressed like a businessman and not a derelict with ripped jeans and a T-shirt.

Now, you might be saying, "I like my ripped jeans and a T-shirt," and truth is, so do I. But I like staying in nice hotels and getting upgraded to a suite for the price of a regular room. It works ... believe me it works! I have stayed in hotels around the world and have gotten upgraded to suites without even having to ask.

ZZ Top made millions by writing a song with a timeless truth — "Every girl's crazy 'bout a sharp dressed man." In turn, I also assure you that every man is crazy about a sharp dressed woman as well. The concept that everyone at Google wears a T-shirt and flip flops is great for Google, but you should not reason by a multibillion-dollar exception to the rule. Step up, dress up, and reflect who you are, what you represent, and doors will open.

Now understand, if you are a personal trainer, I am not suggesting you suit up to go to the gym. However, I am suggesting that whatever profession you are in, it is imperative to dress to your audience to leave the absolute highest impression possible. When you dress to impress, you will be perceived as an authority, a professional, and people will go out of their way to assist you, serve you, buy from you, and want to be  in your company.

Don't use the excuse that dressing nice cost too much money. I never said you had to buy $1,500 Armani suits, a Gucci dress, or Louis Vuitton shoes. You can go to Target, J.C. Penney, Ross, T.J. Maxx, and come out with some great clothes at a very inexpensive price. You can also go on YouTube and watch some fashion experts teach you how to put your wardrobe together.

Stop the excuses, dress up to step up, and wrap the package. When you do, you will experience incredible changes in how you feel, how you are perceived, and how you are received.

Always be a first-rate version of yourself,
never a second-rate version of someone else.

Expose & Close
Marketing System

www.exposeandclose.com

# The Best Calling Card

I learned so much from my dad regarding people skills. My dad was a master networker and had a knack for making friends and influencing people. He used to tell me the best calling card you have is your hand and, if you want to succeed, extend it to as many people as you can, introduce yourself, smile, make eye contact, and deliver sincere handshakes.

I watched my dad, no matter where we were, shake hands with everyone. When he went to a business or networking event, his mission was to connect with each person in the room. He wanted every single person to know WHO HE was, WHAT PROBLEM HE could help them solve, HOW HE could be reached, and WHERE HIS business was located. He mastered the art of the introduction, he mastered his elevator pitch down to a science, and he always carried an engaging conversation building rapport.

Then, he would reach into his pocket and pull out a well-designed business card. This card would properly represent his brand with colors, his logo, and the correct tagline to immediately communicate what business he was in and the problems he could solve. Upon presenting the card to his new friend, he would say, "Here is my card Joe. WHEN would be the best time for us to get together so I can show you HOW...," you can fill in the rest. Bottom line is, it works, it's simple, and you can do it. It's a skill and it can be learned and taught.

The more hands you shake,
the more money you make.

# Powerful Words and Mindsets

# Words are Things

Words are things. They trigger pictures ... which trigger emotions. And when you can say the right words ... that trigger the right pictures ... that trigger the right emotions, then you will get people to take action.

Words are code. Now that we can relate to the importance of software, mobile apps, and the like, we know that if the code is not written perfectly and with a specific intention, the app or software will not perform at the level needed to obtain the solution or objective that you're looking for.

So, I'm here to tell you that you need to become a wordsmith and a craftsman of words. You must learn the right word tracks. You must educate yourself and leverage the power of your words. When you utilize the right words, you will close more deals, shorten your sales cycle, and generate revenue. Let's break down the words 'LEARN', 'KNOWLEDGE', and 'CLOSE'.

Now, this brief exercise might seem very basic, however, words are code with multiple meanings. Words have layers of words and definitions within them. When you say a word to someone, it triggers something in their conscious and subconscious minds. When you put words together properly, it creates rhythm, timing, and flow that can create a positive or negative reaction.

So, let's look at the word 'LEARN'. When you drop the 'L' you have the word 'EARN'. When you LEARN you EARN.

Let's look at the word 'KNOWLEDGE'. I'm sure you have heard the phrase 'Knowledge is power.' KNOWLEDGE is power because when you K.N.O.W. nothing is left to doubt or interpretation. When you KNOW, it gives you the ability to execute and make a decision NOW. It allows you to take time out of your decision-making process and ultimately helps you achieve your objective.

So, when you KNOW you can execute NOW and ultimately CLOSE a deal or solidify an agreement that much faster.

Now here's the kicker. If you can't CLOSE, you LOSE. It's funny how the word 'LOSE' is in the word 'CLOSE'. I interpret the letter 'C' added to the word 'LOSE' to stand for the words 'commitment', 'certainty', 'confidence', 'clarity', 'clearness', and 'comprehensive' — which are all necessary attributes to making a positive presentation and ultimately giving you the ability to build relationships and CLOSE deals.

When you use the right words to trigger a picture in someone's mind, a powerful fusion happens. A picture paints a thousand what ... ?? You know the answer — it's words. The words ... which trigger the pictures ... will trigger emotions. And if the right words are used the trigger will be a positive picture that will communicate and even transcend the right emotion. When people's emotions become powerful and meaningful, it inspires them to make a move and to take action.

It's important to educate yourself and learn the right words and word tracks. When you educate yourself, you elevate yourself. When you educate and elevate yourself, you will educate and elevate your team, employees, customers, kids, and everyone around you. You will be helping yourself more when you educate and help others.

Zig Ziglar said, "You can get anything in life if you help enough other people get what they want." When you help others, you will build more relationships, close more deals, and generate more revenue. When you help others, people will seek you out to buy your goods and services. You become the hot topic — the solution to their problem.

When you educate yourself, you elevate yourself and you will dominate your space. It all begins and continues to grow with the mastery of your words. So, educate to elevate, and elevate to dominate. Pass it on and pay it forward.

Knowledge does not go down in value.

# The "C" Word

When I was 24 years old, I had the honor of being mentored by a gentleman named Jerry Ebstein. This was a guy who was extremely knowledgeable and strategic with business. He taught me many things, but the first lesson was the most important. He called me 'Cinaman' and I called him 'The Jewman'. These were nicknames we had given to each other and were signs of respect and endearment. He always used to say, "Cinaman, listen to the wise old Jew." Which I did, hence the name 'Jewman'.

His first lesson was everything in life boils down to the C word, and when you can master that, you will succeed. The C word is the word 'commitment', and he could not have been more right. Everything you want to achieve in life — any form of success — will boil down to commitment. Having a successful relationship boils down to commitment. Having a profitable business; losing weight; being a great parent, son, daughter, employee; making the basketball team; becoming an actor — it's all about commitment. Writing this book is because of my commitment.

I have had many people ask me, "What level of commitment are you willing to make?" And although there may be different levels of commitment depending on circumstances, The Jewman taught me there was only one level … ALL IN!

When you make a commitment, the word in itself should clearly represent what it truly means. There is no, "Maybe," or, "I'll try." There are no, "If time permits," or, "When I get around to it." There are no, "Well, I don't have the money," "I'm too old," "I'm too young," "I'm too short," "I'm too fat," "I'm too skinny," or, "I don't have a degree."

The commitment represents, "I'll do it," "I will overcome," "I will find another way," "I will go over it, under it, or around it." "I will get up early, go to bed late, and make whatever sacrifices to hit my target."

So many people go through blood, sweat, and tears to achieve their goals and then they stop on the one-yard line. Why would they stop when they are so close to making the touchdown? What a huge and stupid mistake! They fought, struggled, sweat, bled, and just when they were that close, they lost faith and surrendered their commitment. Shame on them! That's right, shame on them! That's not harsh, it's true. Who else should be ashamed if they fall short? They are responsible. It's their fault and they are accountable.

Accountability is the brother and sister of commitment. You need to take accountability for everything you do and don't do. That will help you further pursue and achieve your goals, objectives, and dreams.

When it came to commitment, my buddy Big Vini was a stellar example. Vini was a street guy with a 7th-grade education. However, his vision and drive in life was something that I was fortunate enough to observe and experience firsthand. Vini was not formally trained and educated at the Wharton School of Business. He just had an innate and instinctive entrepreneurial mindset. He knew how to interact with people. All kinds of people. Rich, poor, blue collar, white collar, Black, White, Hispanic … it didn't matter to Vini. He related to everyone and was larger than life — both physically and figuratively.

Vini didn't know what a business plan was or how to build a brand by a textbook perspective, so I guess you can say he wrote his own. He built a multimillion-dollar enterprise and changed the limousine business as we know it today. And he did it by jumping in head first, fully committed, and figured things out as he moved forward.

Although he had no formalized sales and marketing structure, he was marketing and selling 24/7/365. Vini was constantly building a fan base, asking everyone he came in contact with "Hi. What's your name?", promoting himself, promoting his company, marketing, selling, and closing deals. He was constantly making noise and was fully engaged to win. If we left a convenience store, nightclub, restaurant, or toll booth Vini made an introduction and left an impression on everyone he came in contact with. They knew who Vini was, the name of his company, and the product he represented. He was FULLY COMMITTED and a MASTER of EXPOSURE.

One person with commitment
is worth more than a hundred with interest.

# Time: Tomorrow is Promised to Nobody

The most precious resource any human being has in this world is time. The clock is constantly ticking and every breath you take is gone and it will never be given back. Yet so many of us burn time. We burn the heck out of it.

We go to bars with our friends, talk about meaningless things, and put alcohol into our bodies that has no positive attribute to our health. We sit and watch TV or go online and try to live vicariously through the actors and reality stars. In truth, most of the celebrities have no idea how to start a business let alone run a business, sell a product, or be a parent, husband, wife, or mentor.

We try to justify our escape from being productive by saying we are stressed or burned out and we must unwind and relax. However, if we were being productive, generating revenue for our businesses and our family, helping others achieve their goals, and contributing to our communities, we would feel significant, accomplished, and burn out would never come into play.

Everyone needs to have a purpose and feel significant. That's why recognition is something that most people desire more than money. However, this all comes with a price and your key objective must be to control your precious time and not burn it. You do not manage time ... that is a misnomer. You must control it just as if you're driving a car or piloting a plane. You are in control and can press the gas or go full throttle. You can turn left, or right, or change course because you are in control.

Unfortunately, most people never get to where they are going. Not because they don't set goals or because they don't have the education — it is because they procrastinate on BS and burn time. The simple truth is when people procrastinate it's because they have not fully committed to achieve their goal or they haven't taken an action step to make it a priority in their life. When things become a priority, it is amazing how effectively you control the clock.

My father always said to me, "Time waits for no one and tomorrow is promised to nobody." I probably heard that for the first time when I was 10 or 11 years old. I thought I understood it at the TIME. There is that crazy word again. But as that clock kept ticking, the meaning of that phrase took on a new meaning. Let's break it down.

Time waits for no one. You're only 18 years old once. Not twice … once. At 18 you have youth, enthusiasm, curiosity, stamina, and drive. Yet most people will tell you, "You're young. You have plenty of time. Don't be in a rush. Enjoy your life." This is what most of my friends and family members who loved me very much would say to me. However, this was some of the worst advice that I could have been given. I can make more money. I can buy more clothes, more cars, and any other material items, but I cannot get back my most precious resource — TIME!

There are numerous ways to burn time. It is not just about watching a meaningless TV show or watching YouTube. You burn your precious time in ways you may have never even thought about.

My nephew who just graduated at the top of his class was burning time and didn't even realize it. He had been in a relationship with his girlfriend for over two years. It was apparent to every-one around him that he cared for this girl and that he loved her. However, he was not IN LOVE with her, therefore, not commit-ted. I had breakfast with him one morning and said, "Bob, how are things with you and Jen?"

To which he replied, "OK."

I asked, "OK? You have been with this girl for over two years. What does OK mean?"

He continued to tell me what a nice girl she was, how much she did for him, how her family liked him, and blah, blah, blah, blah, blah.

Then, I asked him the million-dollar question, "Are you in love with this girl and do you see yourself marrying her?" Well, you can already guess his response. I proceeded to tell my nephew a few thoughts and shared some advice that I had experienced firsthand.

First, one ounce of doubt … get out. If you are half committed in a relationship, whether it is personal or business, that is a recipe for disaster. Second, how unfair are you being to your-self, how dishonest are you being with yourself, and — just as important from a moral standpoint — how dishonest and unfair are you being to the other person? Now you're burning the other person's time and they will never get it back.

Let me share one of the greatest pieces of advice and insight on relationships I have ever heard. Ready? When your busi-ness goals equal your personal goals, and your personal goals equal your business goals, now you are aligned. Thank you, Jewman. That was one of my first lessons that helped me take a quantum leap in the relationship department.

The message is, if you want kids and she does not, it's going to be a problem. If you want to risk it all and take the jump to open a business and she doesn't, it's going to be a problem. If you work 12-14 hours a day and are fully committed to your financial goals and she wants you home at 5 o'clock for dinner, it's going to be a problem. Make sure your business and personal goals are in alignment and, above all, immediately stop burning time.

How you invest your time is more important
than how you invest your money.

www.exposeandclose.com

# Certainty: A Sales Professional's #1 Job

The word 'certainty' is a very powerful word. It means being 100 percent sure, confident, and established beyond a doubt. It is a word that reflects both knowledge — which is knowing — and the emotion of being empowered. When there is absolutely no doubt that you are 100 percent knowledgeable on a topic and confident of the result a product or service will provide, you will feel the emotion of the word 'empowerment'.

When you are certain you are empowered, and you actually inspire and influence … bringing absolute confidence and conviction to any situation or relationship. You take away any doubt from your mind and the minds of others. That transfers a positive power flow through everyone in your path that you are communicating with. Earlier I used the phrase one ounce of doubt … get out. This holds true for business decisions you must make as well as personal decisions.

Being certain — or the word 'certainty' — is the best $5,000 word I ever paid for.

It was July of 2017, and Grant Cardone was having one of his first sales boot camps in Miami. I met Grant in 2012, when I started selling virtual interactive training platforms. Grant is a client of LightSpeed VT and I had an all-access pass to his Cardone University.

In 2012, Grant was focused on selling his sales training to car dealers and was not the mainstream celebrity he is today. However, I always liked Grant's style and message. I grew up in the sales profession with a lot of mentors who had a similar style and skill sets like Grant. This sales style is a no-nonsense, to the point approach with action steps that if repeated, learned, and implemented would produce results. I tell you all this because when Grant announced his boot camp dates, my uncertainty came into play. Here are some thoughts and self-talk that took place between Charlie Cina and Charlie Cina.

"It's $5 grand. That is a lot of money. What if I get nothing out of it?"

"I know all of Grant's content. What could I possibly learn for $5k?"

"NO, NO, I should go. Proximity is key. If I meet one person I can pay for the trip!!!"

"Oh, go and don't think like a small player. You're being A MISFIT. IT'S ONLY $5K. Plus, it's a write-off."

"What if I don't go? It could cost me thousands in new business?"

"Oh man, I hate leaving Tennille and the kids for 5 days. I should stay home."

These are only a few of the negative thoughts I had, and I could fill another 50 pages of this book with the ridiculous excuses I came up with. However, I called Jarrod Glandt, Grant's VP of sales and said, "Hey man, if you still have room in the boot camp, I want to attend. I'm in. Please send me the info and here is my VISA card."

The conference started at 9 a.m. on July 21, 2017, and, immediately after Grant took the stage, it turned into a sales riff — which is a rapid, energetic, often improvised verbal outpouring and I was picking up what he was spitting out.

Now mind you, I have been in sales all my life. I had trained in my early twenties with Zig Ziglar, Tom Hopkins, Tony Robbins, and others. During my career, I have read numerous books and for the past six years I've worked with, consulted for, or acquired as clients the top speakers and sales trainers in the world. But on that day, at 9:05 a.m., I heard a word I had heard thousands of times before but this time, it put things into a very simple sales perspective and a piece of my mind was ignited.

My job as a sales professional is to sell CERTAINTY. My job as a husband is to sell certainty. My job as a father is to sell certainty. My job as a co-worker, employer, neighbor, or member of the community is to sell certainty. I knew that it was a simple common-sense statement, but for some reason, many of us make the sales process, decision-making process, and the process of building relationships very complex.

In the first five minutes of this $5,000-dollar commitment, I had gotten more value than I could have imagined. I was ready to leave … no joke. My business life and personal life had a new perspective. I got back to my office the following week and immediately scheduled some sales demos.

I hopped on a call with a gentleman and, after a stellar 45-minute presentation on my part by the way, the customer said, "Can you give me a couple days to think about it?"

To which I replied, "Sure, Mike. You could think about it, but you were thinking about it before you called me."

You see, Mike wanted my product, or he would NOT have called me in the first place. I knew he had the money to buy and he was the decision maker. The real issue was Mike was not certain that my product would work for him. Therefore, I had to be more certain than he was that it would work — that it would produce a return on investment.

I continued to verbally knock down his False Expectations Appearing Real (FEAR) and increase his certainty. Needless to say, I closed a deal and got a return on my $5,000 boot camp investment. Further, I realized the importance of continuing to educate myself by attending conferences and seminars to attain knowledge.

No matter what level you are at in life, it's vitally important to get coaching and mentoring. All great athletes like Michael Jordan, Dwyane Wade, and Tiger Woods have coaches. Why? Because they can't take a picture of themselves and get the correct perspective because they are in the frame. It is very difficult to take yourself out of the situation you are emotionally involved in so you can give yourself the clear and effective guidance you need.

Invest in yourself first and always. Have the right mentors, coaches, attend the right seminars, and invest in online training.

If you want to go there,
you need to stay here.

Expose
& Close
Marketing System

www.exposeandclose.com

# Intention and Attention

ntention is a powerful word that is very connected and in alignment with the word 'commitment'. If you're going to make a commitment, you better have the right intentions to back it up and see it through to fruition.

The definition of intention is: a mental state that represents a commitment to carry out an action or actions in the future. Intention involves mental activities such as planning, forethought, and aiming for a target or result. Wayne Dyer said, "Our intention creates our reality."

When I wake up in the morning, it is my intention to expose and close. I must expose my products and services to as many people as I can daily. I must expose the solutions that my products and services can offer to a particular company or individual.

No matter what product or service you provide, it will most likely solve a problem that falls into one of these buckets. Your solution will help them make money, save money, improve their health, improve their financial status, or better their lifestyle. So, here is my intention — my intention is to get your attention. When I get your attention, I want you to pay attention. When you pay attention, eventually you will pay me for my attention.

So, your intention should be to get attention. When you get attention, get people to pay attention, and — eventually — they will pay you for your attention. This isn't a rap or nursery rhyme. Words are things as we discussed in the previous chapters. Words are written code, verbal code, and words are connected. There are word formulas and sequences that, when executed and delivered properly, will help you take quantum leaps. Your end result will be profitable relationships, revenue streams, and a level of success you desire.

There is no one you can't get to if you're determined to take action.

www.exposeandclose.com

# Clients vs. Customers

I don't have customers — I have clients. There's a big difference and you need to know the difference.

The definition of a customer is: **someone who buys goods or services from a business.**

The definition of a client is: **one under the protection of another, dependent, a person who engages the professional advice or services of another.**

I consider myself to be a sales professional not a salesman. I actually educate, elevate, and assist my clients in leveraging the products and services that I provide so they monetize. This allows me to continue to build rapport, build credibility, bring value, and build a long-term revenue relationship. It is important after acquiring a new client to build trust and deliver incredible value. This is a simple way to create a long-term bond.

When someone buys from you, they are usually in a high state of enthusiasm that encompasses numerous emotions, including but not limited to trust, confidence, and excitement. The client ultimately wants to use the product or service they've just purchased from you to achieve their end result. It should be your goal to keep them in the same high state of enthusiasm they experienced at the moment they purchased from you.

It should be your goal to help them achieve their result as quickly and effectively as possible. If this is not achieved, their enthusiasm and belief in your product or service will dissipate, and sometimes this can occur immediately after the purchase.

Once people leave your sales experience and go back to their busy lives, they're looking for the next shiny object that's going to draw their attention. People look for the path of least resistance, even after they have just spent their hard-earned money on a new product or service. All they want is to solve their problem or make their life easier with minimal effort required.

You may have heard the expression you close early, you close often, and you close late. It can also be said that you close in the beginning, the middle, and the end. The reality is you are never done closing. You are never done promoting, marketing, selling, and educating. You are never done Exposing and Closing.

I don't mean to be redundant ... oh, wait a minute ... YES, I DO!

When it comes to creating client relationships for life, you need stick mechanisms and you must create lifetime value fulfilling the needs of your client. If done properly, with the right intention and authenticity, you will connect with your client building a sincere friendship that creates a loyalty that becomes second to none. This loyalty and trust will allow you to sell your client additional products or services, get sincere testimonials, and also get qualified referrals that will result in high-level sales opportunities.

Most salespeople have shallow relationships with their clients after a deal has been closed. Don't be shallow. Make the commitment to swim in deep water and taproot the relationship long term. That single client can reproduce many new relationships and multiple revenue streams.

Remember, whoever says business is not personal is mistaken. Business is very personal. I mentioned it before, your business goals equal your personal goals and your personal goals equal your business goals. If you are not continually building a relationship with your wife, husband, girlfriend, boyfriend, or significant other, I assure you your relationship will not be long term.

Your clients are people and if you want to succeed you must build a relationship. You must communicate with your clients continually. You must celebrate with them on their wins, support them when they have a loss, and essentially bring value to their life. The great news is you can use all the potential million-dollar moves I have shared with you in this book to create clients for life.

Treat people how they want to be treated,
not how you want to be treated.

# When You Expose ...
# You Close!

# You Gotta Move

'Hesitate', 'procrastinate', and 'contemplate' can be very dangerous words in the world of business. They all can be defined as a delay of action.

You may have heard that time kills all deals and ... it's true. You can blame the customer for not buying, or you can make some sorry excuse why they didn't commit, but the reality is it's YOUR fault. It is your responsibility to make sure that they see the value of your product. You must make the customer realize that the product you're offering will last a lot longer than the money that's in their pocket.

The best remedy for closing a deal boils down to one action step — take time out of the process and use speed and persistence to close the deal. Then, implement these five proven steps:

- Follow up
- Follow up
- Follow up
- Follow up
- Follow up

Follow up by phone, follow up by email, follow up by text, follow up by video message, follow up by a personal visit (Hey what a novel idea! Now you're going old school. You're so out you're in.) Send a letter, send a card, or think outside the envelope and send a pizza. The key is to stay top of mind, be diligent, and be consistent in your follow up.

Control time and figure out how to best communicate with your customer. Don't communicate with people how you want to be communicated with. You must figure out how THEY want to be communicated with.

Don't try to close a deal with me by text or email because you're wasting your time. I'm Generation X and I still like closing a deal by phone or in person. I grew up on the phone, made my first million on the phone, and can hear the sincerity or bullshit in the tone of your voice on the phone. Email and text will not do it for me. You send me too many texts and you may even piss me off and you'll never know why. Find out how your customer likes to communicate by asking, "Mr. Customer, what is the best way you would like me to communicate with you — text, email, phone?" You want to do what most of your competition won't.

To help you, I'm going to share some real-life examples of my Expose and Close Marketing System. These tips, techniques, and strategies have helped me close million-dollar deals and acquire some of the top speakers, trainers, and celebrities as clients.

Now is the new later.
Be the 'Right Now' guy or girl.

www.exposeandclose.com

# Organic Money Opportunities

One of my pet peeves in the game of sales, entrepreneurship, and life is that people don't take advantage of the organic money opportunities that are right in front of them.

Everybody is so worried about making a presence on Facebook, Instagram, LinkedIn, or Twitter. A lot of people think social media is the be-all and end-all answer to generating more business, but the reality is it's not and 90 percent of the people on social media aren't social.

Okay … I'll admit that I made that statistic up, but it certainly sounds good and I'm probably not far off. I can assure you that I've met many people from social media and the majority I meet are definitely not social in person — they're Keyboard Warriors. They know how to make an impression or create this persona online, but do they really know how to shake a hand, introduce themselves, and create a real time, in-person relationship?

Now don't misinterpret what I'm trying to convey here. Social media is extremely important, necessary, and it's not going away anytime soon. However, there are opportunities right in front of you. If you make it a point — or better yet a habit — to introduce yourself to just 5 people a day, Monday through Friday, that would result in 260 new potential friendships and/ or business relationships at the end of one year.

Think about it ... when you're at your son's baseball game or your daughter's dance rehearsal ... when you pick up your dry cleaning, you go out for dinner, or you stop at Starbucks, you are crossing paths with people on a daily basis that need what you have. In turn, they have what you need — money and referrals that generates cash flow and revenue.

What I'm suggesting is REAL, LIVE, IN-PERSON social media. There are potential million-dollar opportunities that are right in front of you every day. There are people within a 10-foot radius of you that need to know your name and know what you do. These people need to know how you can help them in their life and business through the products and services you represent. I live by the motto, "The more hands I shake the more money I make." I walk the walk and talk the talk.

This is a true story that happened to me at Grant Cardone's 10x Conference that I attended in Las Vegas on February 22, 2018.

I was walking into the conference at about 9 a.m. and there was a huge line to get in. As I made my way through the crowd, one of Grant's team members recognized me and said, "Charlie, follow me. I'll take you through."

As strange as it sounds, I really didn't feel like fighting the rush even though I had the opportunity to get a fast pass. I told the gentleman thanks, but I really needed a cup of coffee and I would just wait 20 minutes until the line went down.

I walked back into the hotel, sat in front of Starbucks, and opened my laptop. As I sat there catching up on emails, a gentleman and his one-year-old son sat next to me. Now, I could have just kept my head down and focused on my computer screen, however, I can't meet new people if I don't reach out and introduce myself. So, I looked to my right, stuck out my hand and said, "Hi. My name is Charlie. What's your name?" to which the gentleman replied, "My name is Lester."

I said, "Lester, nice to meet you."

Lester replied, "Charlie, nice to meet you. What do you do?"

I said, "I empower speakers, trainers, and subject matter experts to monetize their content online and offline, worldwide, in three easy steps."

Lester said, "Charlie, I need that. Can you help me?"

The short story is, I opened my laptop, gave Lester a demo of the LightSpeed VT platform, and in less than 30 minutes he handed me his credit card for a $5,000 transaction. He also gave me a very compelling testimonial and told me he would introduce me to his mentor who is a successful businessman that owns two hotels in New York and pastors a church of over 70,000 people.

Now it doesn't get any simpler than that. A gentleman sat next to me. I reached out my hand and said, "My name is Charlie. What's your name?" He asked me what I did for a living and I had my power pitch locked and loaded.

I presented myself in a way that was unforgettable at the first point of contact. I positioned myself, building instant credibility and rapport in seconds. And, I profited by creating a client relationship — potentially for life.

Notice my three easy steps ... I PRESENT, POSITION, AND PROFIT.

The techniques and strategies I just explained are very simple, easy to implement, and just require a commitment on your part. Further, this is exactly what I teach to my clients one-on-one, from the stage, and is the key purpose for me writing this book.

Now it's time for you to go out to the world, shake some hands, and build some new relationships.

My New Friend and Client Lester Thornhill
10X Conference - Las Vegas, 2018

Stop manufacturing excuses and take advantage
of the opportunities that are right in front of you.

# The Show Up

One of the techniques I use to 'track down so I can sit down' with a power player is the show up.

It was the summer of 2013, and I wanted to acquire a network marketing company by the name of Kyani as a client. They were having huge growth and had thousands of people in Las Vegas for their national convention. I needed to meet the CEO and introduce him to my online training platform. Unfortunately, I had no contacts at the corporate level. So, I suited up, dressed to impress, and showed up at the event with no ticket, no invite, and no contacts. As I walked to the main entrance of the event the security guard stopped me and said, "Can I help you sir?"

To which I replied, "Yes you can. Thank you so much. My name is Charlie. What's your name?"

She proceeded to tell me her name and I said, "Mary, I need your help. I'm a local resident and represent a business here in Las Vegas. I heard Kyani was having this incredible event and I really need to connect with the CEO as I can help the distributors in this room get better trained so they can increase their retail sales. Do you have any idea how I can connect with the CEO?"

Without saying another word, she walked me through the door, literally pointed out the CEO, and directed me to the area that he was sitting in.

I thanked her and then walked directly up to the CEO and said, "Hi. My name is Charlie Cina. I heard you were having your big national convention and, being based here in Las Vegas, I immediately drove over and wanted to introduce myself and my company."

The short story is, I was able to connect with the CEO who introduced me to their vice president of sales and distributor development. I then had the opportunity to demo my products and services and present them with a proposal to do business.

Now, I would like to tell you that I closed that deal, but I didn't. However, while I was at that Kyani event, I had an opportunity to experience a unique up-and-coming celebrity speaker-trainer named Eric Thomas. At the end of Eric's keynote speech, I walked backstage and introduced myself to Eric. I said, "Hi Eric. My name is Charlie Cina. Pleasure to meet you. Your keynote was outstanding, motivating, and your message was well-received. Let me ask you a question Eric. If I can show you a way to create a virtual online training platform and monetize your content 24/7, on-demand, worldwide, would that be something you would have interest in?"

Needless to say, I got Eric's attention … but he turned out to be a client that was not easy to close. I followed up with him for more than two years. Then, in April of 2017, an opportunity arose where I inked the deal with Eric Thomas, and we launched his Breathe University.

Now, keep in mind, I met Eric at a Kyani event that technically I had no formal invitation to attend, nor did I have any contacts or referrals. No one at the event or at the company knew who the heck I was or what company I represented.

Here's the message … there's power in the SHOW UP! There's networking opportunities in the show up. There's new hands to shake, new people to meet, and new people to greet when you show up. There's opportunity everywhere and sometimes it's as simple as just showing up and being present. When you're present and you introduce yourself and your services you will produce extraordinary results that you didn't even anticipate.

Signed, Sealed, and Delivered
Eric Thomas
"The Hip Hop Preacher"
BreatheUniversity.com

The opportunity is in the show up.

# The Knock

A real example of the knock is when I closed a deal with Jon Taffer, the celebrity host of the TV show Bar Rescue. You know, the guy that throws plates of shitty food at walls and tells the dysfunctional bar owners to, "SHUT IT DOWN!"

I pursued Jon for six months and had been in conversation with numerous people on his staff. I was convinced Jon needed to be on the LightSpeed VT platform and that he could help bar owners worldwide increase their revenues. Well, after six months of banging my head against a wall, I got frustrated and drove to the office Jon had just opened in Las Vegas. I didn't know if he was there and I had no appointment, but I was confident beyond belief he would see me.

As I approached the door, I saw a sign that said, "No Solicitations Allowed." That message had nothing to do with me as I was not soliciting anything. I was there to speak with Jon about a solution that would help him deliver his content worldwide and drive revenue. I rang the buzzer, the lock was released, and I entered the building.

Now, had I been dressed in a ball cap and jeans the invite to enter would most likely have not been possible. As I entered the office, a woman behind the desk said, "Can I help you sir?"

To which I replied, "Hi. My name is Charlie. What's your name?"

She said, "I'm Gina."

"Gina, very nice to meet you. I am here to see Jon. Is he available?"

She said, "No. Do you have an appointment?"

"No I don't, but he will want to see me. I am interested in a potential joint venture and/or licensing his teaching content."

"Well, he isn't here," she replied.

"Then who makes his decisions when he's gone? I need to speak with him or her right away."

Long story short, his Vice President stepped out and I told her how I could help Jon generate revenue online, 24/7, on-demand, worldwide. Two days later, I met with Jon and we had a deal.

I had the privilege to work side-by-side with Jon and his team. We created TVT University, and Jon is now helping bar, nightclub, and restaurant owners increase their revenue by up to 44 percent in just 10 weeks.

The point is, you need to take action and do it right now. Be the 'Right Now' guy or the 'Right Now' girl who will get it done, stand out, be confident, and outshine the competition. Don't wait for the perfect time. Don't wait until you have all the product knowledge. Don't wait for a friend to give you the introduction.

People's priorities are not your priorities. Make the call, get the appointment, set the demo, knock, show up, expose your product, and make the moves that make the difference.

Jon Taffer
Host of Bar Rescue and
taffervt.com

If you don't have a key, then you Knock.

# The Cold Call is Not Dead

Whoever said the cold call is dead is probably not breathing. The question becomes is the cold call the most effective means of prospecting new clients?

In today's day and age, the time of social media, Facebook, Instagram, instant messaging, and all the other forms of communication, the simple answer is no. However, you must use the proper tool or technique no matter how antiquated you think it may be to achieve your goal or end game

I'm here to tell you the cold call is not dead! I closed a high-level reality TV star with what some would call an out-of-date, antiquated cold call. Cold calling with the right strategy, or simply as another point of contact, works.

On April 19, 2009, the first episode of the TV show Cake Boss launched on TLC network. Buddy Valastro — aka 'The Cake Boss' — was the star of the show and it was an absolute hit watched by millions nationwide.

In 2012, I was contracted to market and promote the Light-Speed VT platform and I immediately knew 'The Cake Boss' would be a perfect prospect. I had no direct contact with Buddy and I knew no one in his organization or inner circle. I tried emailing Carlo's Bakery, contacting his agent, and made numerous other attempts to make contact but I kept hitting a dead end. Finally, one day I called Carlo's Bake Shop directly. I said, "I'm trying to contact Buddy. Is he in?"

The person replied, "He's not at this location.

I said, "No problem. What is the best number to reach him at?"

They replied, "Sorry sir, we are not allowed to give out that information."

I said, "Thank you," and I hung up the phone.

As I looked at the phone number it occurred to me that, because they had multiple locations and departments, their phone number could be a rollover number, or they may have a chain of sequential numbers that go to various departments. So, I called the number back, adding a digit to the last number. For example, let's say the last four digits of the main number to Carlo's Bakery was 2001, I would then dial 2002. When a person answered and said, "Carlo's Bakery receiving department," I would hang up and move to the next number.

I dialed 2003 and the person on the other end answered, "Carlo's Bakery sales department."

I dialed 2004, "Carlo's Bakery accounting department."

Then I dialed 2005 and BINGO. The gentleman on the other end of the phone said, "Carlo's Bakery internet marketing. This is John."

I said, "John, my name is Charlie Cina. I hope I'm talking to the right guy. Maybe you can help me. I help speakers, trainers, and reality show stars monetize their content online, worldwide. I would like to talk to you and Buddy about a Cake Boss Online University. Is that something that you think you and Buddy might be interested in?"

Two weeks later, I was on a flight meeting with Buddy and his team to strategize, structure, and design his online program called Baking with Buddy.

This was the true evolution of how I closed this deal. It was through a phone call — a COLD CALL — that led me to use some intuition and common sense, fueled by persistence and tenacity, where I connected with a guy named John, who connected me with Buddy, and I got the deal done. See the cold call was actually a NEW CALL.

Here's the message. You must think outside the box and get creative. You obviously want to use the path of least resistance to achieve your goal, however, you need to utilize whatever tools, techniques, or strategies necessary to achieve that goal. It doesn't matter whether it's old school or new school, will that tool or technique help you win the game?

In this case, cold calling was not dead. A cold call or better yet a new call, allowed me to get attention, deliver my power pitch explaining my value proposition, and elevated me to close a high-level client. So, if someone tells you the cold call is dead, check their pulse. Then pick up the phone and make the call.

Buddy Valastro
'The Cake Boss'
In the LightSpeed VT Studio

Don't equate challenge with loss.

Expose
& Close
Marketing System

www.exposeandclose.com

# Direct Mail is so "Out" It's "In"

I remember when direct mail was a major form of advertising, a major form of communication, and a major form of getting your marketing message into households and businesses nationwide. Then came the internet, internet marketing, Facebook marketing, and other forms of social media marketing that virtually (no pun intended) eliminated — or least drastically decreased — the number of direct mail ads sent out by businesses.

Well, I'm here to tell you that direct mail is so out that it's in.

Now, I don't mean to be redundant, but you must understand that no method of contact, exposure, or introduction is outdated. You must focus your energy and strategy on getting attention in any way, shape, or form. I have closed sizable six and even seven-figure revenue relationships by implementing and sending out a very simplistic direct mail piece.

When I was in the construction industry, I represented a floor leveling company that's sold self-leveling cementitious underlayment. Essentially, we repaired interior concrete floors. My market was high-rise condominium projects in Las Vegas as well as existing and new hotel-casino projects on the Las Vegas Strip.

I knew if I was going to enter this market, I had to align myself with the right affiliate partner who would plug me into their business relationships and would make me a part of their team. That affiliate company was Superior Tile & Marble. They contracted hundreds of millions of dollars in flooring jobs throughout Las Vegas and on the Las Vegas Strip.

The gentleman at Superior Tile & Marble who decided what contractors (affiliate partners) to use was Steve Scolari. I sent Steve a flyer that represented my product, I attached my business card with a green paper clip, and I put everything in a white legal-sized envelope.

Now, I'll be the first to tell you that this mail piece was nothing special. Quite frankly, it was not my best work. But it was functional, and it communicated my message. So, I personally addressed the envelope with some of the worst handwriting known to man and hoped for the best.

Three months went by and not a word from Steve.

Now keep in mind, I followed up with Steve by phone and email to confirm he received my mail piece; however, he never took my calls or emailed a response. Then one day out of the blue, I get a call from this rough deep voice on the other end that said, "Charlie, this is Steve Scolari. I've been looking at your flyer that's been in the left-hand drawer of my desk for the past three months. I have a job for you right now if you have the ability to get it done. How quick can you get to my office?"

Now I can't make this up, but I was literally less than two blocks from Steve's office when he called. I proceeded to keep him on the phone by asking him questions about the project as I drove straight to his office.

When I walked into his office unannounced, I looked him in the eyes and said with a smile, "Steve, is this quick enough service for you?" He looked up at me, smiled, and called me a smartass. We immediately proceeded to look at the plans, I wrote a proposal, and we inked a deal.

So, a simple flyer with a simple clear marketing message sent directly by mail that literally cost me less than $0.67 including postage resulted in a project at the Wynn Resort that produced an excess of $2.5 million dollars in revenue. That's right, $2.5 million baby, and a long-term revenue relationship progressed from there. More projects, more contracts, and more revenue.

The point is, marketing doesn't need to be expensive or complicated, it just needs to make an impression and be effective. Shout from the rooftops if you have to and make sure you promote your product or service, so people know what you do.

So, let me ask you three important questions:

Is this simple? Yes.

Does it work? You bet!

Can you do it? Of course, you can!

That simple mail piece was an impression that kept me TOP of MIND with the decision maker. That simple move helped me build my brand and allowed me to be that person's first phone call when he needed the products and services that I provided.

Just remember that your marketing doesn't have to be fancy to be effective. Just take the action steps and implement.

This $0.67
Unattractive Investment

Resulted in a Grand Slam

High tech or low tech,
high touch results in high checks.

www.exposeandclose.com

# The Drop Off

The whole concept of the drop off is utilizing the same sales collateral used in your direct mail piece, packaging it a little bit different, and changing the delivery method.

With the drop off, instead of putting a stamp on an envelope and having the mailman deliver your direct mail piece, you get in your car and personally show up to deliver it. By showing up, you can potentially meet with your point of contact in person to present and educate them on your products and services.

Now, the actual example I'm about to share utilizes the same flyer and business card that I used to get the Wynn Resort deal and I added a sticky note that said, "Call me when I can be of service." The only difference was, I personally dropped it off in a 9-inch by 12-inch pocket folder. I walked into this company named Turnberry Partners and said to the receptionist, "Hi. I'm Charlie. Is Steve Kessler in this morning?"

To which the receptionist said, "He's in a meeting."

I said, "Please give this to Steve and let him know I'm available immediately to start working on any upcoming projects he may have."

A couple of days later, I received a call from Steve who said he was organizing a project and had some questions about my product and install procedures.

He said, "I normally use another company, but your folder was on my desk and the other contractor didn't return my call."

How sad the other contractor had poor follow-up skills. Bad luck for them and good luck for me, right? But it's not luck at all. It's about being persistent, consistent, and resilient. It's about implementation and taking action. It's about follow-up and follow through. Think about it. Dropping off some marketing material and answering my phone the first time the customer called resulted in a 10-year relationship that generated millions of dollars in sales. Now, think about the contractor that lost millions of dollars because he didn't return a call.

Turnberry built six high-rise condominiums in Las Vegas and the $4.5 billion-dollar Fontainebleau resort. Unfortunately, the recession hit, and the Fontainebleau was never completed. However, it was an incredible run and implementing the move of the drop off was effective and profitable.

When you Expose, you Close. Your objective is to keep it simple and always be delivering TOMA — Top of Mind Awareness.

Not Fancy BUT IT WORKS!!!!

Marketing does not need to be fancy,
it just needs to be functional.

# Video Follow Up

I t's a known fact that people would much rather watch a video than read a long email message. In addition, the open rates for emails are not promising. For example, if you send 100 emails and 10 of them bounce, this leaves you with 90 delivered emails. Of those 90 emails, let's say that 10 are opened. This means that your email campaign open rate is 11 percent (10 emails opened from 90 delivered). For this reason, I have implemented the use of a video email-video texting service.

The first thing I love about video email is that I can send out many more messages, more effectively, and with more emotion and meaning. Another big factor is video email is five times more effective than me typing out and sending a text email message. Further, I can send five video messages in the same amount of time it would take me to physically type out one.

There are numerous reasons video email and video texting are more effective, but I will give you the top five.

- Video allows you to display nonverbal communication. Body language and verbal tone play a huge role in conveying the message. Text content relies on precise word choice and punctuation — which is not always a person's strength — and takes a tremendous amount of time to complete.

- Video engages your audience. With the combination of

sound and visuals you can immediately captivate a person's attention and get viewers to listen as long as you are delivering valuable, authentic, and concise content.

- Video is simply much easier and more convenient for your viewers to consume and understand.

- Video insights action. Because your video implies high tech with high touch, combined with your authentic message designed to emotionally connect, people are more apt to respond to your call to action.

- Video is king. We are living in a video first world where social video is becoming the heart of everything.

Here is a real-life example that took place in February of 2018, by using video email.

I closed a $25,000 deal with a major player that I hadn't been in contact with for quite a while by just sending him a 33-second reconnect video. Here's the script of what I said on the video.

"Hey Rod, Charlie Cina. I hope all is well. I just wanted to reach out — you were top of mind. I was in San Francisco over the weekend watching the Olympics and you and Apollo popped to mind. (The gentleman I was recording the video for is partners with eight-time Winter Olympic Speed Skating Medalist, Apolo Ohno.) I just wanted to reach out and see how you were doing. I hope things at Alysian are going well and would love to connect for a call and catch up. I would love to show you the advancements that we have made here with the technology as well. So, let me know what your schedule is looking like. Shoot me a text or call me anytime. I look forward to speaking. Thanks."

That's it. Simple. No $10,000 words. Just a quick authentic video letting him know that he was top of mind — and it only took one take. Check out the actual email thread between Rod and I on the next page.

Re: How Are Things

On Feb 12, 2018, at 3:32 PM, Charlie Cina <charlie.cina@ light-speedvt.com> wrote:

On Mon, Feb 12, 2018 at 9:57 PM, Rod Jao <rod@----.com> wrote:

Hi Charlie.

Allysian is doing well. We also started another major project in the block-chain space.

Please check us out.

Good to hear from you.

Warm Regards,
Rod Jao
CEO, Co-Founder

On Feb 13, 2018, at 12:25 PM, Charlie Cina <charlie.cina@ lightspeedvt.com> wrote:

Glad to hear from you and I will check out hybridblock. I just launched a company on the LightSpeed VT platform that is in this space by the name of Ormeus. They are having incredible success.

All the best on your new venture and if I can be assistance let me know.

Now, here's the kicker. I sent the video email to him on a Monday and responded back to him on Tuesday. On Friday evening of that week, while I was out to dinner with my family, I received a phone call from a gentleman by the name of Henry. He said, "Charlie, I'm associates with Rod and Apolo. I'm in Vegas this weekend to celebrate Chinese New Year. I would love to meet with you to discuss your online training platform and see if there is an opportunity for us to do business."

Now, I want you to keep something in mind. The day I sent Rod that email, I had made the decision to go back and look at all the prospects that I had not contacted in the last 12 to 24 months — deals that most people would have thought were dead, never to produce any type of revenue relationship. And, with a 33-second video using very authentic and simple language, I was able to generate $25,000 of initial revenue that also produces for me a monthly recurring revenue stream.

The video email tool costs me $49 a month and it is the best $49 a month I've ever spent.

So, ask yourself again today, and ask yourself again tomorrow. Ask yourself even when you don't feel like asking yourself the following questions: Is it easy? Does it work? Can I do it?

I don't have to tell you; you already know the answers. Come on, let's make it happen.

Rod Joa and Eight-Time Olympic Medalist Apolo Ohno

Persistence is another word for faith.

# Exposure Tips and Techniques

**118** Expose and Close

# Send a Note, Send a Card, Send a Pizza

Creating multiple points of contact, staying top of mind, thanking people, showing people that you remember them, celebrating them, and having the authentic intention of building a relationship are paramount in life and in business. I personally make it my mission to send people personal notes, birthday cards, thank you cards, send flowers, and I've even been known to send a pizza.

It's really simple ... people like to be recognized, people like to feel significant, and everybody appreciates an authentic friendship whether it's personal or business. Many people say business is not personal, but nothing could be further from the truth. Business is definitely personal. It's my profession, it's what I do, it's the product and service I represent. It's how I feed my family. It's the value that I provide to the free market. So, business is definitely personal, and I make it my job and my duty to make sure that my clients become my friends.

Now, some people may disagree with that, however, I'm here to tell you that it has worked for me. Most business relationships I build result in friendships and ultimately result in long-term revenue relationships. These long-term revenue relationships also produce abundant referrals that are ultimately qualified prospects and dream clients.

So, here are some great tools and moves that I use to stay top of mind and to let my friends and clients know they're appreciated.

After you've met with a client for a personal meeting, a lunch, or dinner, send a personal note recapping briefly what was discussed and let them know how much you appreciate the relationship.

Send a card for a birthday, wedding anniversary, business anniversary, or whatever celebratory event that may be going on in that person's life at that particular time. I use a service that allows me to custom make cards by incorporating photos of the person I'm sending the card to. The service also allows me to send candy, brownies, cookies, and other various gifts with the card.

I used this service to send a thank you to one of my good friends and client Anthony Delmedico. Anthony is the founder of Storm Ventures Group and he hosts a yearly conference called Win the Storm for over 2,000 roofing contractors.

Last year, he invited me to speak at his conference and deliver my Expose and Close marketing message. After the event, I sent him a personalized card and brownies. Now, Anthony is a very successful businessman and he has the money and wherewithal to buy anything he chooses. However, when a man of his caliber picks up the phone to express how genuinely appreciative he was to receive a thank you card with a box of brownies, you really start to realize that it's the simple things that people truly appreciate.

I have also utilized this service and marketing strategy to get people's attention. I have a list of the top people I want to prospect. Sometimes emails, video emails, texts, knocks, and show ups just don't work. In these cases, I'll send a card. I will custom make a card with a picture that complements that individual and their business. I'll put their company logo on the card as well. Again, the objective is to get people's attention and one of the main ways is to show them a picture of themselves.

So, when they open the box, there is a card in it with their picture on the front. Inside the card is a Starbucks gift card and a message that says, "I have been trying to connect with you for a cup of coffee. The coffee is on me, just let me know when you can carve out 15 minutes for a call. Look forward to speaking soon. Charlie."

Although nothing works 100 percent of the time, this million-dollar move gets me pretty darn close. I can get somebody's attention and schedule a 15 to 20-minute uninterrupted call. Now I have their full attention to educate them on how I can solve their problems, help them reach their goals, and generate more revenue.

Anthony Delmedico's
Thank You Card with Brownies

It's nice to be important, but
it's important to be nice.

www.exposeandclose.com

# Social Media and Facebook

One thing I'm not is a social media guru. I'm not proud of that because social media is an absolute must as far as Exposing and Closing. It's an incredible opportunity to get attention, show people who you are, and advertise your brand, your products, and your services.

Now, to be completely transparent, I have a hard time with social media because so many people broadcast their message that aren't really qualified to do so. I'm not judging or hating, it's just sometimes there's so much noise I don't know if I actually want to participate. However, I have come to the realization that you have to be in the game no matter what. The reality is, even though I am no social media expert, and even though I don't do the amount of posting that should be done, it has still been extremely effective for me.

Social media is a must and it's not going away anytime soon. Therefore, I would suggest you follow and learn from the social media gurus of the world and leverage these extraordinary media outlets. That said, I'm a perfect example that even if you're not doing everything 100 percent right, the exposure you get can give you a 100 percent positive result.

Last year, I did a Facebook Live and was telling the story of how I acquired Jon Taffer as a new client. That Facebook Live resulted in a 21-year-old emerging motivational speaker showing up at my office. There was a knock on my door and one of my associates said to me, "Charlie, there's a young guy here by the name of Andy. He said he saw you on a Facebook Live and he's in the conference room. He would like to meet you. Do you have a minute?"

I was swamped with back-to-back calls and executive briefings, but I realized if this young man took the time to drive four hours from Los Angeles to implement the show up, I owed him the courtesy of an introduction and handshake. When I walked into the room, I introduced myself to this very well-groomed and polite young gentleman. As we started our conversation, I leaned over a bit perplexed and said, "How do you know me? Have we ever met before?"

He said, "No we haven't. I actually saw you on a Facebook Live telling your story about how you just showed up at Jon Taffer's office and closed that deal. I was so impressed and inspired I really wanted to take the time to come down here and meet you personally."

That's when it really hit. Social media is a marketing, advertising, and communication beast. It works … end of story. Andy made me realize firsthand the impact each of us can have on the world by sharing our stories, our knowledge, and our talents.

Since meeting Andy, we have built a friendship and I have had the privilege to mentor him on his quest to become a speaker and businessman. During one of our many conversations about sales, Andy asked me what's the real secret to acquiring clients like Les Brown, Jon Taffer, and so many others. My response to Andy just flowed off my tongue. I said, "Andy, I just Expose and Close. I take every opportunity to introduce myself, hand out my business cards, make follow-up calls, send emails, and do whatever it takes to stay top of mind and close a deal.

Andy immediately replied, "Charlie, I'm doing an event called the Southern California Sales Conference. Les Brown will be speaking there as well as numerous other experts in their fields. Would you consider speaking at my event and introducing my audience to your Expose and Close Marketing Concept?"

So, on September 29, 2017, I had the opportunity to present my Expose and Close keynote speech. Sharing the stage opposite one of the greatest speakers of all time, Mr. Les Brown, was truly an honor. From that event, I got numerous other speaking gigs and acquired new clients on the LightSpeed VT training platform. I have also done several Expose and Close webinars, acquired consulting clients, and have been prompted to write this book. The past 12 months have been incredible, and I have forged many new friendships, business relationships, and opportunities. Why? All because I shared my story on social media.

It's time for you to share your story. Let the world know who you are, what you do, and how you can help people and businesses solve their problems. Social media is a powerful tool and the sky is the limit ... or better yet, there is no limit.

"Shoot for the moon. Even if you miss,
you'll land amongst the stars."
—Les Brown

Engaging in Social Media is a must. Never underestimate the impact your story can have on another person's life.

www.exposeandclose.com

# Voicemail and Text Messages

There's nothing more frustrating than making a cold call, a follow-up call, or any call for that matter and the person doesn't pick up on the other end. I've had days where I have literally made hundreds of calls and the majority resulted in listening to a voicemail.

Working in high-level sales environments my entire life has introduced me to various frustrations when teaching both new and experienced salespeople. That said, it drives me insane when people do not leave voicemail messages.

Think about it for a minute. You've done all the work by dialing the phone, listening to the voicemail message, and then you hang up without leaving your message. Now, I am here to tell you that in today's day and age, some people — including myself — don't always listen to their voicemail messages. However, what about the people who do? There is your opportunity. Also, many people now have their voicemails converted to digital voicemail text messages, which is a huge benefit as text messages covert better for a call back.

Remember, a voicemail is another opportunity to make an impression. It is another form of advertising, marketing, and promotion. It doesn't take longer than 10 seconds for you to leave a voicemail message. If it's a cold call, you should have your message down pat and be able to recite it with clarity, conveying a compelling call to action. For example, "Joe, this is Charlie Cina. We need to connect and discuss how I can help you and your sales team increase revenues by potentially 20 to 30 percent in the next 30 to 60 days. I'm working with companies in your arena like Dell, Mitsubishi, LG, Verizon, and others. My cell is 702.555.1212. I look forward to hearing back from you."

Now, this is just an example, but I'm sure you get the picture. The next thing I do is pull out my cell phone and send a text message and an audio text message with the same verbiage. These are simple steps that take just a little bit of extra time and effort. The result, however, is you left another impression, another reason to be top of mind with that particular individual and company. It's another form of repetitive advertising. The same message delivered by a different form of media.

So, if you dial the phone and get a voicemail recording, leave a message with a clear value proposition and call to action. If you do this consistently, I guarantee you will get a profitable result that you're looking for. It may not happen immediately, but over time it will help you acquire a positive revenue relationship.

All methods of contact must be used in order to achieve extraordinary success.

Expose
& Close
Marketing System

www.exposeandclose.com

# Million Dollar Messengers

We have all heard that word of mouth is the best form of advertising. I agree with that statement 100 percent. When someone tells you about a product or service they love and you can hear and feel the emotion in their voice and see the emotion on their face and through their body language, this is a display of truth, authenticity, and proof in its purest form.

People live vicariously through the opinions, thoughts, and actions of other people. So, how can you take control and duplicate this powerful process? How can you implement a system where you can deliver an actual client's results and experiences based on word of mouth advertising?

The process is actually simple. I call this form of advertising the Million-Dollar Messenger. Imagine if you could obtain authentic referral messages and deliver them through social media, at live events, on your website, and through various other marketing outlets.

What I'm about to share with you is replicable, duplicatable, and sustainable. This technique, or strategy, will allow you to emotionally connect with your audience whether they are potential prospects or existing clients. The technique I'm referring to is the power of client testimonials. Testimonials that are short, precise, and tight. Testimonials that will help you overcome objections before a potential client even asks.

The right video testimonial will allow you to deliver a marketing message that will help you create a virtual money machine. Your prospects can hear firsthand the experience, emotional connection, and solution you are prepared to deliver right from the mouth of a satisfied client. A testimonial should be in your client's own words conveying their personal experience, thoughts, and results that your product or service has provided.

Remember this … everything falls under feeling. People buy products to make them feel good. People buy products or services to solve a problem. People buy a product or service because they want return on investment. Once that problem is solved for your client, it will trigger an emotional feeling. This is not theory, it's fact.

The best time to get a testimonial is when your clients are in state … meaning a happy, high-level emotional mindset of complete satisfaction.

Here are a couple important pointers when asking a client for a testimonial.

When someone gives you a testimonial, make sure they use your first and last name.

If they have made money with your product or service, make sure they get specific. For example: "As a direct result of Charlie Cina's teachings and using the Expose and Close Marketing System, I closed a $10,000 sale in my first week."

Now that's a great testimonial. However, providing tangible proof with a testimonial is even better. In this example, tangible proof would be a copy of the check for $10,000 with the date. Another example of tangible proof might be a before and after picture of someone losing weight. The important thing to understand is there cannot be a testimonial of theory, it must be fact.

Testimonials are there to celebrate the success of your clients as a direct result of using your product or service. By celebrating your client's success, you essentially pique people's interest and they become emotionally compelled to learn more about your product, or better yet, are prepared to buy your product on the spot.

Your new objective and hobby should be to obtain as many testimonials as possible from your clients. It's best to get a testimonial from a client immediately after you have helped them solve a problem or they have purchased your product or service. Simply look them in the eye and ask, "Would you mind if I take out my phone and capture a quick testimonial of you expressing how you feel about how I have helped you here today? It will assist me to better help people in the future."

It's a simple process and most people are happy to say some kind words about you and the product or service you represent. The more you do this, the more proficient you will be at getting short effective testimonials that will make all the difference in your business. Trust me, more testimonials will result in tremendous dollars.

Here are some testimonials from my actual clients.

"Charlie Cina has been my sales consultant and mentor for the past 5 years. From just one coaching session alone, and using Charlie's strategies, I was able close $26,000 in one day. My biggest day ever, period, end of story. Charlie, thank you, I love you, and I hope you can help others just like me."

Mickey Hernandez
Sales Manager
LaceUp Solutions Software

"We brought Charlie in to speak and deliver his Expose and Close System, it was amazing. We had people coming up to us and saying he was one of the best speakers we had, and his delivery was phenomenal. He's a great speaker and it was an awesome night. We would love to have him back again."

Chris and Lorissa Naugle
The Flip Out
Real Estate Academy
flipoutacademy.com

"We engaged Charlie Cina to help us increase sales and generate revenue. I refer to him as my behind the scenes secret weapon. He brought to my team specific sales techniques and phrasing to help us drive sales. I love working with Charlie and look forward to more success in the future.

Shep Hyken
Fortune 500 Speaker
Author of *The Customer Focus*
shepardvirtualtraining.com

To access examples of video testimonials,
simply scan this QR Code

People live vicariously through the
thoughts and actions of others.

# Nothing Falls on Deaf Ears

named this chapter Nothing Falls on Deaf Ears for a reason. Many of us try to call, text, email, send cards, knock doors, and prospect in any way, shape, or form possible to make a sales contact. It can be a long frustrating process, and at times you think your efforts are going unnoticed. You feel like all the noise you are making is falling on deaf ears. Not true. You are absolutely, positively making an impression. Everyone is watching, listening, and sometimes — depending on your industry — may be touching, smelling, and tasting what you have to offer.

Now, that may sound strange or awkward, but it's all by design. We all have five senses which are sight, hearing, taste, smell, and touch.

Let's say you put up a billboard (sense of sight) on a highway — which some people consider old school. Not true. On any given day, tens of thousands of people drive down the I-15 North from Southern California to Las Vegas. This means that each day the billboards that line the highway receive tens of thousands of views, which in today's day and age are known as impressions. Now, it may be hard to identify exactly which customers walk into a restaurant, clothing store, or hotel because of these billboards, but they do provide positive exposure.

The same thing can be said for a radio ad (sense of hearing). If a radio ad is done properly, with a clear marketing message and a compelling call to action, you can positively measure the results of that radio ad and establish your return on investment. In addition, you will also acquire many new clients because of your radio ad that you may not be able to quantify. The shear exposure and repetition of hearing your name through radio will cause you to stay top of mind with potential clients and, eventually, they will walk in your door to do business.

If you are a restaurant, bakery, or coffee shop, you might give out free samples (sense of taste) of your product in front of your store. The delicious aromas (sense of smell) that come from your place of business can also trigger positive emotions that make people want to come in and try the delicious edibles you have to offer.

And then there's the sense of touch, which is one of our most powerful senses. If you have a product that can be demonstrated in some way, shape, or form and you can physically put it in the hands of your potential client, your closing ratio will go through the roof.

I try to incorporate the five senses into my Expose and Close process. However, there are numerous instances — after all the attempts and creative efforts to make a contact and close a deal — that I feel like a complete failure. I feel like all my efforts are being ignored. I'm here to tell you firsthand that this is not the case. You're planting seeds and sometimes it is hard to see the actual growth that is going on beneath the soil. You have to stay consistent in your mission, you have to be persistent by making all the moves, continuing to follow up, and follow through.

Here is an example of an email I received from a gentleman by the name of Jeffrey McGee. Jeffrey is one of the top sales trainers in the country and brilliant at what he does. I wanted to collaborate with Jeffrey and help him create his online training platform so he could monetize his content worldwide. I utilized every move and technique that I've shared with you in the book to make contact with Jeffrey. I also experimented with various other moves to get his attention. To be honest, I thought Jeffrey didn't like my product, didn't like my approach, or maybe flat-out didn't like me. However, I found out by surprise that nothing could be further from the truth.

After almost a year of no return correspondence, I was shocked when Jeffrey finally contacted me, and I was even more shocked to discover he was referring me to a high-level client.

Jeffrey's email had a subject line that read:

**"Re: Email Introduction/Immediate Business Development Opportunities Between You Two."**

In the email, Jeffrey facilitated an introduction between me, and a gentleman named Sam and encouraged us to connect ASAP. Jeffrey went on to describe me as a colleague and a gentleman that he had known since 2013. He said that I represented a lot of his friends and colleagues in the professional development space and helped them develop and launch their online training platforms.

After reading this email, I sat at my desk and reflected on the numerous attempts I made to connect with Jeffery. I sent him emails, made numerous phone calls, left him voicemails, video voicemails, and texts, always trying to remain top of mind. I thought I had failed in my attempts, but what you will see in the following email is the social proof that Nothing Falls on Deaf Ears.

Run hard and fast to achieve your objectives. Many obstacles will cross your path, you will get blocked on numerous occasions, and you will feel mentally and physically beat up. The key is to keep moving and don't stop at the one-yard line. People are listening, people are watching, and when they are ready and need your services, you will be top of mind and building new revenue relationships.

The email I received from Jeffrey is on the next page.

Re: Email Introduction/Immediate Business Development Opportunities Between You Two!

 Jeffrey Magee drjeff@-----.com 9/20/17

Charlie Cina and Sam Palazzolo –

Gentlemen,

Let me facilitate an e-Introduction and encourage you two to connect ASAP …

1. Sam Palazzolo is a longtime colleague and friend that now lives in LV … He is a Venture Capitalist that has launched a new business that engages automotive dealerships nationally.

2. Charlie Cina is a colleague and gentlemen I met when I moved to Vegas in 2013, he is with www.lightspeedvt.com and has a lot of my friends/colleague's professional development IP on-line with their LMS system … More importantly the Founder of LightSpeed is big in and from the automotive industry, along with Charlie …

You all need to talk; I see a lot of immediate collaboration and business opportunities within …

Best wishes!
Dr. Jeffrey Magee,
CMC, CBE, PDM, CSP

When you think no one is listening, it's
time to perform, persist, and persevere.

# CONCLUSION
# There's No Silver Bullet

I n the world of promotion, marketing, and sales there is No
Silver Bullet that guarantees you will make a sale and close
the deal. When people start to promote, market, and engage
in the sales process, most quit before they even get to first
base. To be a true sales professional you must understand who
you are marketing to and what problems your product can help
those people or businesses solve and overcome.

Each one of your potential prospects has their own DNA or their
own dynamic needs, wants, and personalities. They all have
different characteristics, their own mindset, and thought pro-
cesses that make them tick. They also have their own priorities,
both on a business and personal level.

A person's priorities will often hinder or slow down your sales
process. Understanding people's personalities, priorities, and
learning what ultimately makes them feel comfortable is the key.
The objective you must achieve with any prospect is to quickly
connect, convey, and collect.

You must CONNECT with a person quickly, so you make an
incredible first impression. You must CONVEY your marketing
message where you become the solution to their problem.

Then, you can dramatically increase your ability to COLLECT a new revenue relationship.

Unfortunately, you cannot always connect, convey, and collect at your first point of contact. You may be able to connect at your first point of contact and do it effectively, but you probably will not be able to fully convey your message or offer and close a deal to collect money at your first point of contact.

Achieving the three Cs during your first point of contact isn't impossible, but it's highly unlikely. Based upon your price point, most sales require 7 to 10 points of contact before a customer commits and the exchange of money occurs. Therefore, I want to impress upon you there is no silver bullet. To achieve the sale you must treat people how they want to be treated. You must focus on what is important to them. What problems do they want to solve? What are their objectives? What are their goals? Can your product or service help get them there?

Be ready to put numerous bullets in your verbal arsenal, your written arsenal, your video arsenal, and be prepared to implement touch marketing … which means getting in your car to personally visit a prospect, shaking a hand, or taking a client to lunch or dinner. Set up a free webinar to educate your prospects on how they can leverage your product or service to achieve their end game and increase revenue. Be ready to execute all the potential MILLION-DOLLAR MOVES I have shared with you to EXPOSE and CLOSE. These moves are EASY to implement, these moves definitely WORK, and you CAN put them into action and achieve success.

It has been my pleasure to share with you my tips, techniques, and strategies that have allowed me to generate millions of dollars and provide a lifestyle for my family where we continue to pursue our goals, dreams, and reach our objectives. I want to encourage you to make a positive impression and leave a positive impression with every person you meet.

In closing, continue to educate yourself on this extraordinary profession called sales. Use every road, opportunity, relationship, tool, and technique to get to the bank.

For a free download and gifts:
Visit me at www.exposeandclose.com

Be stubborn about your objectives
and creative with your execution.

# Resources

**Check out my favorite tools I use to stay top of mind.**

**The following companies have 'Affiliate Programs' in which I participate.**

**Greeting Cards & Gifts**

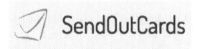

**SendOutCards.com/222446**

**Video Email & Text**

**BombBomb.com**

# My Digital Business Card

My Best Friend, Trusted Confidant
and
Love of My Life, My Wife Tennille

June 8, 2018, Corinthia Hotel
London, England

www.exposeandclose.com

# Thought Leaders, Influencers and Mentors

The Real Brad Lea
CEO LightSpeed VT

Dr. Nido Quebein
Speaker, Author, Businessman
President of High Point University

Rita Davenport
International Speaker & Author

Grant Cardone & My Son Carmen
Cardone Enterprises

Anthony Delmedico-CEO
Storm Ventures Group
svguniversity.com

Jim Doyle, John Hannon
Jim Doyle & Associates
doyleondemand.com

Kevin Harrington, The Original Shark
As Seen on TV Titan

Mr. Les Brown
Top 10 Best
Motivational Speaker in The World
lesbrownunlimited.com

Sharon Lechter
Speaker, Author, Entrepreneur

Dr. Tony Alessandra & Shep Hyken
drtonyvirtualtraining.com
shepardvirtualtraining.com

Dr. Aaron Gumm
Speaker, Author, Coach
blueprintuniversity.co

Special Thanks To

Joel Bauer
Speaker, Trainer, Infotainer

www.exposeandclose.com

Made in the USA
Middletown, DE
24 January 2020